# Culture and Biology:
## Becoming Human

GARY G. TUNNELL

University of Montana
Missoula

Burgess Publishing Company  •  Minneapolis, Minnesota

1    2    3    4    5    6    7    8    9    0

A SERIES ON
BASIC CONCEPTS IN ANTHROPOLOGY
Under the Editorship of
A. J. Kelso, University of Colorado
Aram Yengoyan, University of Michigan

# *Contents*

# The Cultural Concept

It is generally accepted that *Homo sapiens* is the only animal that has culture. There are other animals, however, that in one form or another approach cultural behavior. Chimpanzees seem to be able to learn a "language" of over one hundred "words" consisting of plastic symbols (Premack and Premack 1972) or signs made with the hands and fingers (Gardner and Gardner 1969). They have also been observed plucking sticks, preparing, and using them to fish for termites (Lawick-Goodall 1967), and there is indirect evidence that they use "clubs" and rocks to shell nuts in some areas and not in others (Struhsaker and Hunkler 1971). Japanese macaques have been observed washing sand off potatoes after observing other animals doing the same. Further, potato-washing mothers passed the habit to their offspring (Kawai 1965). Sea otters swim on their backs in the water with rocks on their chests and use the rocks to crack molluscs (Fisher 1939). Intuitively all of these behaviors seem to be similar to human cultural behavior. Two important themes are present: tool use and language. Yet, we only have to think of the incredible complexity of human cultural behavior to realize that there are important differences.

There have been many definitions of culture that have been used by anthropologists in their investigations. The variety in these definitions is partially the result of the necessity to define cultural behavior in a way which facilitates their research objectives. Common elements seem to exist in these definitions, however, and it is these we will look at in our attempt to understand the relationship between culture and biology.

One primary element often found in definitions of culture is that culture is learned behavior. A second element is that learned patterns are passed from one generation to another. For our purpose then, we can think of culture as dependent on man's ability to learn and pass learned patterns across generations. Man's ability to pass learned patterns across generations is closely related to his linguistic ability. The problem of the origin of culture is, thus, closely tied to the problem of language origins.

In their attempts to explain human social structure and function, social

1

scientists have often chosen culture as the attribute making man different from the rest of the animal kingdom. In the last century when the social sciences were still in the process of separating from philosophy, the biggest problem to be solved was how to sort out the biological from the cultural. It was becoming obvious from the writings of Darwin and others that man had animal and earthly origins. He ate, he slept, he copulated, he resembled the apes in body form, and in the end he died and decomposed. It was equally as obvious that man was unlike any other known animal. He had table manners, he slept in a bed, he wrote love poems, he wore clothes and had religion to explain away death.

Darwin's theory of natural selection provided a mechanism whereby all life including man could have come into existence without divine decree. Western theologists through two thousand and more years had said there were two types of creature: animal and human. God had created the animals and he had created man to watch over and use the animals. The theory of natural selection said that man, just like all other living creatures, had come into being because of reproductive success. Darwin had spent many years cataloguing the variation that exists in all species. Dogs, for example, come in all sizes from two to two hundred pounds, several colors and mixed, with short, medium, or long hair and so on. Since many more creatures are born into the world than survive long enough to reproduce, why *do* some survive? They must compete with each other for available food and other necessities of life. Some variants survive; others do not. The ones that survive reproduce and pass on their characteristics to their offspring. Then, the whole process begins again with the offspring. Given extremely long periods of time and a source of new variation such a mechanism could explain existing life forms. Geologists in Darwin's time were discovering the great antiquity of the earth, so the time was available. Geneticists in this century have found the source of totally new variation at the chemical level: mutation.

Actually scholars had been thinking and writing about evolution for many years before Darwin's *The Origin of Species* was published in 1859. A French botanist, Jean Baptiste Lamarck, published a book in 1809 in which he suggested that traits could be acquired directly from the environment. His *Philosophie Zoologique* (1809) was actually just a presentation of ideas that were common at the time. Darwin's grandfather, Erasmus Darwin, was among those who suggested that evolution through the inheritance of acquired characters could take place. The acquired character idea is the one illustrated *ad nauseum* with the giraffe example: the giraffe stretches his neck to reach higher leaves to eat and because of this exercise passes on a longer neck to his offspring. This idea has long since been rejected by biologists but is of interest to us here for one reason: culture *is* Lamarckian. The experiences a person has in his lifetime are stored as memories in the brain. These experiences can be passed on through language or imitative learning to offspring. The long developmental period of human infants facilitates this learning process. Biological evolution is Darwinian; culture is Lamarckian.

Sir Edward Burnett Tylor, one of the founders of anthropology, gave the following definition of culture in his *Primitive Culture*:

*Culture or Civilization, taken in its wide ethnographic sense is that complex whole which includes knowledge, belief, art, morals, law, custom and any other capabilities and habits acquired by man as a member of society. The condition of culture among the various societies of mankind, in so far as it is capable of being investigated on general principles, is a subject apt for the study of laws of human thought and action.* (1871)

Tylor's reference to the "capabilities and habits acquired by man as a member of society" contains the elements precipitated earlier in the paper from other definitions, namely: learned behavior passed across generations. He does not relate cultural variation to biological variation in *Homo sapiens*. This is a critical point since the infant social sciences were at this time just beginning to see that the two were not causally related. It is easy to understand why this sorting out of culture from biology was so difficult: the people of the world differed in body form, skin color, etc., and they also differed in their customs, beliefs, and morals. To see the two as causally related would seem to follow. Beginning with Tylor (though he also was somewhat racist by our standards), anthropologists could examine man's cultural variation separately from his biological variation or race.

# Nature/Nurture

## INSTINCT AND LEARNING

The problem of distinguishing culture from biology in human social behavior is only one facet of a philosophical problem that has been around since the early Greeks. This is the nature/nurture problem. Is individual behavior attributable to biological nature and built in or is it the result of the sociocultural and wider environment acting upon a standardized biological substrate? One can find extreme views either way in philosophical debates through the centuries. Locke, for example, in his *Essay Concerning Human Understanding* (1690) saw man as *tabula rasa*, a blank slate to be written upon by the environment. A similar, often quoted view from this century was expressed by J. B. Watson, an early behaviorist:

*Give me a dozen healthy infants, well-formed, and my own specified world to bring them up in, and I'll guarantee to take any one at random and train him to become any type of specialist I might select—doctor, lawyer, artist, merchant-chief and, yes, even beggar-man and thief, regardless of his talents, penchants, tendencies, abilities, vocations, and the race of his ancestors.* (1930:104)

The opposing view of man as the product of innate proclivities has often taken as extreme a turn. William McDougall (1923) from the same time period felt that a man's life was shaped by a number of different instincts:

1. Instinct of flight
2. Instinct of repulsion
3. Instinct of curiosity
4. Instinct of pugnacity
5. Instinct of self-abasement
6. Instinct of self-assertion
7. Parental instinct
8. Instinct of reproduction
9. Instinct to collect and board things
10. Instinct of gregariousness
11. Instinct of construction

These arguments about man's "nature" go on and on. The nature/nurture controversy has, in fact, continued to the present.

## BEHAVIORISM VERSUS ETHOLOGY

B. F. Skinner, one of the great psychologists of our time, argues not that biological elements have no influence on human behavior but that compared to environmental contingencies they are simply unimportant. Konrad Lorenz, the ethologist, argues conversely that behavioral scientists have ignored the biology of behavior at great risk; man may destroy himself because he failed to understand his aggressive nature. Here we have two great modern scientists telling us that man is in trouble. He is in trouble because he does not understand why he behaves the way he does. They both call for action in solving environmental and social problems. One feels that we have failed because we have not understood man's biological nature. The other feels that we have failed because we have too often seen man as a biological entity. Whom are we to believe? How can we extract ourselves from these arguments and yet use the insights into human behavior that these two lines of thought have given us?

The nature/nurture issue can be attacked by logical argument. If we reduce it to the absurd the either/or dichotomy disappears. Thus, where do we find an organism that has developed in the total absence of an environment? Only with such an organism could we hope to demonstrate totally innate behavior patterns. Likewise, how can behavior be expressed at all in the absence of biological organisms? If we argue that human behavior is due totally to either nature or nurture we have to accept there can be behavior with no organism or that an organism can develop in the absence of an environment (Thiessen 1972:2).

Men of the stature of B. F. Skinner and Konrad Lorenz certainly understand this logic as do most behavioral scientists. The problem is that the logical argument tells us only that there is no either/or question. It cannot tell us the relative contribution of nature and nurture, of biology and the environment. The debate is over the significance of biological and environmental factors in the final product of child development: the adult personality. The debate is likewise over the relative importance of these factors in the collective behavior of men as social beings who possess and are shaped by their culture. We will look at these two bodies of thought briefly and then show how the nature/nurture dichotomy is being dissolved by some researchers.

Konrad Lorenz is an ethologist. Ethologists stress the study of behavior in a naturalistic setting rather than in a laboratory. They often supplement field observations with laboratory checks on certain facets of natural units of behavior. They are interested in the evolution of behavior and thus the function of behavior patterns in the natural setting. Their goal is to accumulate a behavioral inventory called an *ethogram*. This is a catalogue of

5

the behavior patterns of an animal. Ethologists have most often studied animals but recently have attempted to apply their techniques to the study of man. This attempt has been criticized by many behavioral scientists because they feel that man is not an animal and that techniques developed for animal studies should not be used with humans.

Since ethologists have mostly been concerned with animal behavior, they are interested in innate behavior patterns. They have developed a number of terms for use in explaining these patterns and their function in an evolutionary perspective. These terms are somewhat technical but become meaningful when applied to examples. The basic unit of behavior in ethological analysis is the *fixed action pattern*. The term is descriptive. It refers to a pattern of behavior that is inherited or is learned rapidly in a critical period. It is stereotyped and usually shown in the same context. Each fixed action pattern is motivated by *reaction specific energy* which builds up in the central nervous system until the animal finds itself in a situation appropriate to the acting out of the fixed action pattern. This situation is usually one in which a particular signal called a *configuration of sign stimuli* serves as a *releaser* for the fixed action pattern. There is, in the central nervous system and perceptual system of the animal, a *receptory correlate*. This receptory correlate is in classical ethology a built-in sensitivity to particular features of the environment or the configuration of sign stimuli. As reaction specific energy builds up the animal may show *appetitive behavior*, that is, it tries to bring itself into a situation in which the fixed action pattern can occur. If the animal is unable to put itself in an appropriate situation it may *release in a vacuum*. It may show the fixed behavior pattern in the absence of the appropriate context (Lorenz 1970, 1969, 1965).

Examples give these terms much more meaning. This writer has observed typical vacuum activity in a pet mongrel dog. The dog was reared indoors and fed only dry or canned commercial food to the age of one year. At that time she was observed with some regularity burying imaginary tidbits. The action seemed to be released by the yielding softness of an overstuffed chair that the dog slept in. She would dig furiously at the soft leather upholstery, place the imaginary tidbit (perhaps a bone?) in the imaginary hole and push imaginary dirt over it with her nose. She would then defend the area viciously, though she was seldom hostile otherwise. The action was the same time after time but ceased and was never repeated when the dog was introduced to a change of address, real bones, and real dirt.

Numerous examples of fixed action patterns are available (see Eible-Eibesfeldt 1970). There seem to be some examples from human behavior that fit the classical ethological scheme. A human baby seems to have a *receptory correlate* for the perception of eyes. It will smile even at two large dots on a card which serve as releasers of the smile (Spitz and Wolf 1946). The smile then supposedly releases mothering responses in the adult. Bowlby (1969) in a book on mother/infant relationships has shown that "mothering" has a number of patterns of this type. These mechanisms help in the formation of bonds between mother and offspring that could have been of great value in the preservation of the species. Another ethologist has done a cross-cultural study of facial expressions using slow motion film to record the results. He "...found agreement in the smallest detail in the flirting behavior of girls from Samoa, Papua, France, Japan, Africa (Turcana and other Nilotohamite tribes) and South American Indians (Waika, Orinoko)" (Eible-Eibesfeldt 1970: 416). They smiled at the person, lifted their eyebrows with a quick movement, then looked down or away, often with a laugh or smile of embarrassment. Controlled laboratory experiments have shown that recognition of some facial expressions is innate in nonhuman primates. G. P. Sackett, for example, raised rhesus monkeys in isolation from other monkeys from birth until nine months. They were shown slides of landscape, geometric figures, other monkeys, etc., then taught to project the slides according to their own preference. They preferred looking at other monkeys. One of these slides was of a threatening adult. Suddenly, at two and one-half months of age, they showed fearful responses to this picture. They greatly reduced the number of times they showed this slide thereafter. This response occurred without the experience of other animals (Sackett 1966).

Ethologists have also described another phenomenon in animal behavior that may be applicable to humans. *Imprinting* is an evolutionary adaptation characterized by rapid learning of special responses. It takes place during a sensitive period in the developmental process and results in memories that are present for life. Forgetting usually occurs with other types of learning unless the learned patterns are reinforced. Another characteristic of imprinting is that the animal learns only supraindividual species-specific characteristics (Eible-Eibesfeldt 1970:229-230). The organism is not open to any kind of information during the sensitive period, only specific types. Konrad Lorenz discovered imprinting. His geese imprinted on him during the sensitive period. They would follow him but not the mother goose. They would also follow any other human. The specific type of learning they were open to was whom to follow. When they fixated on man rather than goose, any man would do. Imprinting may be important in human language learning as we will see later.

B. F. Skinner is a behavioral psychologist and an extremely influential and controversial scientist. We will look at his psychology not because it is representative of the field but because of his accent on the importance of environment. Behavioral psychology can be seen as an attempt to explain behavior by what is observed rather than calling on "mentality." A mental explanation is one that attributes behavior to instincts, feelings, purposes, wills, or other qualities possessed by an organism. Behaviorists feel that such explanations are dead ends. Saying that an infant nurses because it feels hungry does not lead to further inquiry. They would replace such explanations with descriptions of responses to stimuli. The response to the behaviorist is the equivalent of the atom to the physicist or the cell to the biologist in that it is the basic unit of analysis:

*We can follow the path taken by physics and biology by turning directly to the relation between behavior and the environment and neglecting supposed mediating states of mind. Physics did not advance by looking more closely at the jubilance of a falling body, or biology by looking at the nature of vital spirits, and we do not need to try to discover what personalities, states of mind, feelings, traits of character, plans, purposes, intentions, or the other perquisites of autonomous man really are in order to get on with a scientific analysis of behavior.* (Skinner 1972:12-13)

"Stimulus" comes from a Latin word meaning "to goad" and "response" comes from a Latin word meaning "to answer." A stimulus and a response can be defined by the behavioral psychologist to suit the needs of his research program. The two terms can be defined in terms of each other. A stimulus is something which brings a particular response under certain conditions and a response is how an organism reacts to this stimulation. Learning is thought to take place as an organism reacts to different stimuli. Some behaviorists think that any human behavior that cannot be explained by stimulus-response learning is inconsequential. Thus, one should be able to take any well-formed infant and, by controlling his environment, make him into whatever one wishes.

Skinner's own view is that responses have consequences. We are never sure in seemingly spontaneous nonlaboratory behavior what stimuli brought the observed response. He feels, however, that this is unimportant. What is important is the consequence of the response, especially when learning takes place as the result of this consequence. His system is known as *operant conditioning*. It grew out of experiments with rats and pigeons in boxes outfitted with special feeding devices. A lever could be pressed by the animal to dispense a food pellet. The first push of the lever resulted from an unknown stimulus. Who knows why a rat pushes a lever? As a consequence of this response to an unknown stimulus, a food pellet is dispensed and quickly eaten. If the *schedule of reinforcement* is continuous, every time he pushes the lever he gets a pellet. The pellet is known as the *reinforcer*. A continuous schedule should lead eventually to the animal greatly increasing his rate of lever pushing. The *strength of the response* can be measured. The response can also be *extincted*. If the food pellet is no longer delivered with the push of the lever the animal will eventually return to the response strength preceding reinforcement. The behavior of the animal is being controlled by manipulating the environment (Skinner 1961, 1953, 1938).

Operant conditioning can be used and has been used to explain many different kinds of animal and human behavior. Skinner and a number of other behaviorists feel that behavior modification through operant conditioning should be used in shaping human society. They have succeeded in developing operant techniques for the treatment of many behavior disorders from temper tantrums to psychoses. While they feel that behavioral genetic and ethological factors may exist, they feel that they are inconsequential in comparison to learning through reinforcement. Free will is nonexistent. Man only reacts to external stimuli.

In the views of Lorenz and Skinner we surely have polar views. Both have urged that man is doomed because of the other's view. (See *On Aggression* by Lorenz and *Beyond Freedom and Dignity* by Skinner.) Both have the support of vast amounts of conclusive research to support their views. One advocates nature and the other nurture as the prime mover of human affairs. How are we to find a route between Scylla and Charybdis?

## UNTYING THE NATURE/NURTURE KNOT

In solving this problem our first assumption will be that all behavior has a genetic component because there can be no behavior without an organism. This comes from our earlier reduction to the absurd of the nature/nurture argument and an *a priori* rejection of vitalism, the soul, and "ghosts in the machine." There can of course be no genes that are for behavior alone. Behavior is secondary to structure and genes for structure. To say there are no genes for behavior alone does not mean, however, that structures have not come into existence because of selection for behavior patterns. Organisms actively interact with the environment and behavior can be adaptive or maladaptive. Selection for behavior at the behavioral level changes structures and/or their functions. It is impossible to divorce structure and behavior. They are two facets of the same reality. Our second assumption will be that behavior is related to the environment in two different ways. (1) It originally arose through mutation and evolved by natural selection (and other evolutionary mechanisms that bring changes in the gene pool) to fit the environment. (2) In the developmental process of each individual the environment interacts with the genetic component to produce the behavior or morphology that we observe. A geneticist would put it in the terms shown in the diagram on the next page.

We said earlier that culture is learned behavior that is passed across generations. If culture is learned behavior, how can it also be genetic? Is this

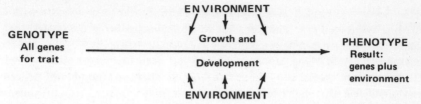

not a contradiction? It is not because the ability to learn is inherited. Learning ability has a behavioral genetic base and seems to vary in individuals just as height or weight or finger length varies between individuals. (Refer to Manosevitz, Lindsey, and Thiessen for a catalogue of human behavioral genetic variation and ways of investigating it.) Since the ability to learn has a behavioral genetic base and shows variation between individuals, there is no reason why this should not have been true quite early in hominid evolution. It is easy to see how natural selection could have acted on this variation to produce the learning ability necessary for the origin of culture.

A number of selection experiments have been done with animals for "intelligence" phenotypes. These indicate that results can be obtained just as easily for behavioral traits such as intelligence as for morphological traits. An early experiment of this sort was published by Tryon in 1940. He started with a heterogenous group of rats and selected for breeding the "brightest" and the "dullest" based on their ability to run a maze. He let the brights mate only with brights and the dulls only with dulls. He then selected again the brightest and the dullest from among these offspring and so on. The divergence was immediate and continued through the seventh generation after which there was little further change. The animals had apparently been selected to the limit of the existing variation. Further change would have called for mutation to provide new genetic possibilities. Later evidence indicated that the "brightness" selected for was related to particular sensory cues. However the "bright" and the "dull" lines still exist and show obvious differences in their performance in different mazes.

The evidence that variation exists in *Homo sapiens* for intelligence comes from the numerous studies that have been done using I.Q. tests. There are many vexing questions to be asked about the validity of these tests as indicators of innate general intelligence. Slater and Cowie in a recent review of the subject say:

*Some educationists have taken the view that the innate contribution to intelligence is a small one, and that the relatively low intelligence which has been found to be so much commoner in the children of unintelligent parents has been caused by the deficiencies in early upbringing. The child in his first few years picks up a great deal in the way of vocabulary from his parents and sibs, or in the case of dull and inarticulate families, very little. Despite all the efforts that have been made to purify the assessment of this contribution from the early environment, a certain element is bound to remain. Nevertheless, tests have been improved so far that, in the best test for this purpose, the genetic contribution to variance is larger than the environmental one, in some estimates by a factor as large as 4:1.*

*Regarding I.Q.'s for the purpose of the present discussion, as moderately accurate estimates of innate general ability, one can see how far the known facts about their distribution in the population correspond with available genetical models. The distribution of I.Q.'s fits fairly well with the normal curve. . . .* (Slater and Cowie 1971:189)

Further evidence that intelligence has a fairly high genetic component comes from twin studies. Identical twins are identical genetically. Studies have been done in which identical twins who had been reared separately were tested for I.Q. Even though they had been reared separately they scored closer together than nonidentical twins that had been brought up in the same household. (See Erlenmeyer-Kimling and Jarvik, 1963, for a review of fifty-two studies of intelligence in relatives.) We can probably accept then that intelligence has a fairly high genetic component. At this time there is a fairly wide variation in intelligence. It has been suggested that when quite a bit of variation is shown in a trait the trait is not under intensive directional selection. Otherwise the variation would be decreased because a portion of the variants would be unable to reproduce. This variation may be due to civilization acting as a buffer. An individual would have to have an extremely low intelligence to be unable to procreate. Projecting many years into the past it is probable that selection did act on intellectual phenotypes. It is not hard to imagine how.

Our first assumption, then, is that even the higher intellectual functions in man have a behavioral genetic base. Man learns but his ability to learn depends partially on the neurological equipment he inherits. What he will learn also depends on motivational factors, personality factors and so forth, many of which also show behavioral genetic variation. What the person learns, the rapidity of learning and so forth depend on what responses are reinforced by the environment, unless we are talking about special types of learning such as imprinting. Our second assumption, again, is that the environment interacts throughout the developmental process with the behavioral genetic base. The genotype, or all the genes having to do with a particular trait, interacts with the environment to produce the phenotype. The phenotype is the observable result in either morphology or behavior after the action of the environment on the genotype. An analogy with a computer can be used. Imagine a very special type of blueprint that not only has all the information about how a type of computer is to be built but actually directs the construction! This blueprint can represent all of the genes that an individual carries. Now imagine that this computer actually starts to function at an early stage in its construction. All kinds of wiring and electronic parts are provided from the environment and assembled according to the instructions of the blueprint. We have the equivalent here of food intake in a biological organism, metabolism, and the construction of organs from the resulting chemical building blocks. But let us further suppose that the elaborating computer is also being programmed from the very start. It is being given instructions about the kind of actions it can take and this information is stored in its memory banks. In fact this information will to some extent determine the wiring patterns of the memory banks. The resulting computer will be the product of the blueprint that directed the construction, the quality and availability of materials used, and the quality and availability of the programming as the construction proceeded. What will be the nature of this machine? Is the "behavioral" output the result of the blueprint or the program? It would appear that possibilities for output will be limited by the overall construction plan. An analog computer will not become a digital computer because of the program. The output possible will also depend, however, on all the information stored during its construction and up to the present (Figure 1).

Cultural behavior is learned behavior but what constraints and forming elements are there on the course of culture that derive from man's neurological equipment? Some anthropologists have suggested that these constraints may be of considerable importance to the understanding of cultural universals—patterns found in all or almost all cultures such as incest taboos, the nuclear family, religion, mythologies, etc. Tiger and Fox suggest:

*In the same way,* all *the rest of human culture lies in the biology of the species. We have a* culture-acquisition device *constraining us to produce recognizable and analyzable human cultures, just as we must produce recognizable human languages, however varied the local manifestations may be. Just as a child can learn only a language that follows the "normal" rules of grammar for human languages, he can learn only a grammar of behavior that follows the parallel rules of the biogrammar. Of course, in either case, a departure from normal grammar may be tried, but the likelihood is that it will end only in gibberish.* (Tiger and Fox 1972:13)

Other anthropologists have suggested that culture is based upon man's ability to symbol and that this ability is unique to man. They feel that since culture consists of a body of these symbols, biological constraints are presently unimportant in sociocultural evolution. Man's cognitive apparatus serves collectively as the carrier of culture but culture itself consists of the

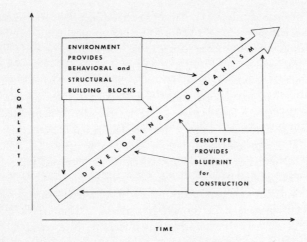

**Figure 1. Genotype and environment interact as the organism develops.**

symbols. These symbols interact among themselves to further elaborate and thus culture evolves. This is a suprabiological, cultural deterministic view of culture and social organization. Leslie A. White is probably best known for this view:

*Within the human species there is a great variety of social organization. Consequently (and here is a very important point that is often overlooked), there are two fundamentally different kinds of sociology: (1) the sociology of nonhuman species, which is a subdivision of biology, and (2) the sociology of human beings, which is a subdivision of the science of culture, or culturology, because it is a function of this external suprabiological, supraorganic tradition called culture. This is a fundamental difference between the social organization of man and the social organization of all other creatures.* (White 1973:10)

This view is very different from that of Tiger and Fox quoted earlier.

Actually, the two views of culture may not have to contradict each other any more than we have to view the individual as the total result of either nature or nurture. Culture exists now. If we accept that it did not always exist and that man evolved biologically to his present complexity in relation to other organisms, then culture must have come into existence as the result of biological evolution. When culture reached certain levels of complexity it may well have taken on a dynamic of its own as symbols interacted with symbols. The new element in cultural evolution would not necessarily countermand the evolution of cultural capacity though this might occur with the arrival of civilization. Even then biological constraints could exist over and above the interaction of symbols. For example, tribal groups all over the world tend to number around five hundred individuals. It has been suggested that this is about the number of people that the average person can relate to on a first name basis (Pfeiffer 1972:375-379). This could well be a constraint based on human cognitive capacity.

Symbolic interactions have recently come to be known popularly as "spinoffs." This term was first used for techniques or artifacts generated by space technology that were of use in other fields. It has since come to be used to refer to the unforeseen uses of new ideas in general. For example, the development of the laser beam revitalized three-dimensional photography or holography. Holographic techniques are in turn revolutionizing information storage and retrieval. Holographic information storage has further suggested a model for distributed memory storage in the brain! The laser beam concept obviously held different possibilities for different researchers according to their own cognitive makeup. Likewise, if one researcher in neurophysiology had not been familiar with holographic concepts another would have been. The concept would certainly have been used sooner or later because of the interaction of concepts. (See White 1973:32-39, for a clear and concise coverage of this idea.)

While animal studies have to be generalized to humans with care and reservation there is an older experiment with mice that shows the subtleties of nature/nurture interactions. Calhoun used two different inbred strains of mice with different dwelling preferences. One strain preferred apartments built above ground and the other dug small burrows below the ground. He took newborns from each strain and placed them with a mother of the opposite strain. When they were weaned they were placed in colonies with others of the same strain. His object was to discover if the dwellings they built were culturally or biologically determined. The cross-fostering prevented social learning of the trait. His first observation was that the apartment mice piled their diggings and the burrow mice did not. After twenty generations the two strains had completely resumed their home building techniques (Calhoun 1956).

Cultural anthropologists have thoroughly demonstrated that a member of any human "race" is capable of becoming a fully functional member of another society and a participant in their culture. The results of the above experiment are given to suggest that propensities may well exist to learn some types of information better than others. These propensities are, however, part of the ethogram of *Homo sapiens* and not of any particular race of *Homo sapiens*. It is likely that we can learn more about these basic constraints and propensities by studying not only cultural universals but human paleontology and the human brain. We will turn to these in the succeeding chapters.

# Cultural Paleontology

The direct evidence for human evolution comes from fossils. The paleoanthropologist provides this evidence by directing a team of scientists and technicians in the recovery, preservation, and interpretation of fossil hominids. Without these data from the past, theory could tell us little. Enough hominid fossils have been found, however, to give us some idea of the major events in human evolution. Theory from genetics, ecology, geology, and anthropology allows the paleoanthropologist to string the fossils together in likely phylogenetic patterns. Since so few fossils have been found and since there are gaps in the fossil record there are an unfortunate number of phylogenetic schemes available for us to choose from. This is true not only because of gaps in the fossil record but also because of the diversity of theory available, i.e., ecological theory may suggest one interpretation and geological theory another. Luckily, a large number of scientists are at work on problems of this kind and better data are being interpreted in the light of analysis of complete systems. Theories from different research areas are no longer being seen as separate but as supplementary.

For our purpose, the simplest phylogenetic scheme available will do (Figure 2). We are especially interested in two items within this scheme. What changes have occurred in the brain? How has culture as evidenced by tool use changed through the same time period?

Australopithecus lived at least five million years ago in east-central and south Africa. They lived on the ground, walked erect, and probably fed themselves by scavenging, gathering food plants, and hunting small game. Tools over two million years old have been found in Australopithecine sites. These consist of crude stone flakes and choppers that seem to have been sharpened by knocking off flakes. There may have been two species of Australopithecus, or the different fossils could simply represent different sexes. They seem to have ranged from four to five feet in height and probably weighed between 80 and 140 pounds. Judging from existing primates they likely lived in small groups and traveled over a fairly large territory. Their cranial capacity ranged between 435 and 540 cubic centimeters which is somewhat larger than the chimpanzee's 400 cubic centimeters. It has been suggested (Hewes 1971) that

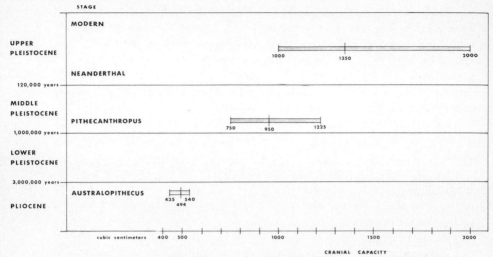

Figure 2. Hominid phylogeny showing range of cranial capacities. Neanderthal and Modern are lumped. The range for *Australopithecus* is for *africanus* only. (Cranial capacities from P. V. Tobias, *The Brain in Hominid Evolution*. New York: University of Columbia Press, 1971.)

they had a linguistic ability beyond that of any existing nonhuman primate. This may have consisted of both gestures and calls.

The second stage of hominid evolution is represented by the pithecanthropines. These fossils are classified as *Homo erectus*. They are of the genus *Homo* and are considered to have been true men. These fossils have been found in Africa, China, Java, and Europe and have been dated between one million and five-hundred thousand years. They are possibly represented in east-central Africa much earlier. This is the *Pithecanthropus* stage of hominid evolution.

They indicate a larger brained hominid of between 740 and 1225 cubic centimeters cranial capacity. Crude chopper-chopping tools have been found in association with these fossils as well as fireplaces containing charred animal bones. Sites with no hominid fossils but much cultural and faunal material have been found in Spain and dated at around 300,000 years before the present (Howell 1965:85-100). These sites, attributed to *Homo erectus*, indicate that organized hunting of big game was taking place.

Looking much like enlarged *Homo erectus* skulls, Neanderthal crania show the upper cranial capacity in hominid evolution with a mean of 1470 cubic centimeters. These fossils have also been found in Africa, Europe, and Asia. They were present between 110,000 and 35,000 years ago and are now classified as *Homo sapiens*. They were excellent hunters and tool-makers and there is evidence that they had a religion.

Truly modern man arose about 35,000 years ago and probably evolved in some areas before others. The Neanderthals disappeared shortly, the result of both cross-breeding and an inability to compete with modern man. The cranial capacity of moderns varies widely from area to area and even within populations but seems to average somewhat less than that of the Neanderthals. Cultural evolution has been greatly accelerated since the advent of modern man. Present-day artifacts range from stone tools to space vehicles. Hunters and gatherers still exist but a greatly increased world population depends primarily on the use of fossil fuels in farming for high agricultural yields.

In the above thumbnail sketch of hominid evolution we can see several trends. There is an increase in cranial capacity, an increase in variety and skill of tool use, and a change from scavenging and gathering to big game hunting and gathering and finally to food production. A body of theory in use by many anthropologists suggests that these changes in culture and in morphology developed in a feedback relationship to each other through natural selection. Perhaps the best "summing up" of this body of theory has been done by Bielicki (1969:57-60). We will use his trait complexes, which he feels evolved together and represent the essential elements in hominid evolution, to make sense of what we know of existing fossils.

His first element is (1) erect bipedal locomotion. This is followed by (2) brain size and complexity, (3) noncyclic sexual receptivity of the female, (4) retardation of ontogenetic development or simply the long period of childhood, (5) hunting, (6) tool using and tool making, (7) symbolic communication, and (8) certain characteristics of social organization such as mating rules and within-group economic cooperation. He sees the biological and the cultural elements above as related in a special way: they amplify each other through time. Increasing tool use could bring a selection for increased brain size. In turn, increased brain size would make more complex tool use possible and likely. Noncyclic sexual receptivity of the female caused by hormonal changes and certain types of changes in social organization might also develop in the same way. Constant receptivity would help in integrating groups but also make mating rules necessary. Mating rules might well lead to stronger male/female relationships which would be further cemented by further increases in receptivity. It is possible to see a number of such "feedback" relationships that could have existed between sets of the above elements in hominid evolution.

It is unfortunately impossible to measure behavior directly from fossil material. As we saw in the last chapter, however, both behavior and morphology are best seen as facets of a single reality. They can never be entirely split apart. Though behavior patterns of the past have been lost in the sense that the behavior itself was short-lived, these patterns can be inferred to some extent from morphology. A physical anthropologist can look at the fossil pelvis and femur of *Australopithecus* and see that this hominid walked bipedally. He can look at the bony crest along the top of the skull of one variant of *Australopithecus* and hypothesize from this one bit of information that it ate large amounts of vegetable matter. The sagittal crest serves as a muscle attachment area for a muscle that moves the lower jaw. The existence of the sagittal crest indicates that this muscle was well developed. It was probably not related to defensive behavior since large canine teeth were not present. It may have been present then because this variant *Australopithecus* ate large amounts of vegetable matter. There are many clues of this type that he may look at and other information will be used to supplement these clues. If he suspects one variant of *Australopithecus* may have been a vegetarian, the first question he must ask is whether it has ever been found with animal bones. If it has, is there evidence that they represent killed or scavenged creatures? He will want to know something about the ecology of the area when the creature lived. If it was a desert at the time, vegetable foods may have been rare; this would necessitate changing his hypothesis.

This is the kind of reasoning that is done in trying to understand the evolution of the brain and the relationship of changes in the brain to changes in culture and behavior. Fossil skulls show that the brain has at least tripled in size during the last three million years (Figure 2). It is also likely that evolution has brought a reorganization of the brain. Reorganization of the brain is not something that can be measured from the fossils themselves because there are no fossil brains. Much evidence from the fields of neurology, ethology, and comparative psychology must be used, then, to clothe the bare fossils in behavior. (See Tobias 1971, and Holloway 1968, for summaries of what is known about the evolution of the brain and statements on methods of study.) While culture can be considered on a level of its own without reference to biology, the origin of culture cannot be productively investigated in this way. The evolution of the brain and the origin of culture are intimately related.

# Culture and the Brain

## BRAIN ORGANIZATION

The brain and spinal cord make up the central nervous system in man. The central nervous system takes in information through the sense organs via the afferent nerves. It controls the movements of the body through the afferent nerves by causing muscles to contract. One can think of it as a functional unit with a number of subsystems that have more specialized chores. As a functional unit within the body it is in charge of receiving information about the environment, processing this information, retaining for the future what may be of use, and ultimately acting upon the environment through muscular control. The environment can be external or internal; it can be outside of the body or inside the body. To say that it receives information from the internal environment and acts upon it is simply to say that it controls such bodily functions as hunger and thirst. Our special interest will be in language, tool skills, and the ability to symbol in the brain of man since these are largely unique to man and are responsible for his culture-related behavior.

The brain is made up of a number of structures that have been found to have specialized functions. The picture is anything but simple, however. It is not a question of one circumscribed area taking care of one function in most cases but of one area being implicated along with others in the performance of a function. Many researchers are working on various aspects of neurobiology and there is still much to be learned. We are largely ignorant of the operation of many behavior patterns at the neurophysiological level. The exact nature of memory storage is not even known. There are a number of hypotheses that seem to fit the observations but it is not yet possible to choose between them with any certainty. There may even be a number of memory mechanisms. A vast accumulation of knowledge about the brain has occurred, and some of this knowledge can give us direction in our search for the biological basis for cultural behavior.

In the phylogenetic sense, man has three brains. The structure and organization of these brains come to man through his heritage as a creature

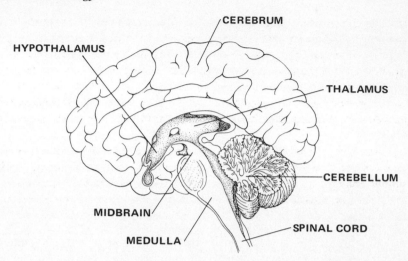

**Figure 3. Side view of bisected brain. See text for explanation.**

that has evolved. The oldest part of the brain can be called the reptilian brain because it is similar to the brain of living reptiles. Over and around this brain is built the old mammalian brain and over and around it the new mammalian brain (MacLean 1968:24-34). The earlier structures are the more basic to survival. The later structures are more involved in complex memory processes and ultimately, in the cerebrum, consciousness. The reptilian brain (Figure 3) includes the medulla which controls breathing, swallowing, digestion, and heartbeat. It contains areas important in telling man when to be alert and when it is safe to leave his conscious mind turned off. An important switching center called the midbrain is also part of the reptilian heritage. It not only switches and directs incoming information for the rest of the brain but takes care of certain reflexes such as the enlargement of the pupil of the eye in darkness and sudden closing of the pupil in bright light. The reptilian brain takes care of very basic functions such as mating and breeding. In man, of course, these also have a conscious component. The old mammalian brain is known as the limbic system. It contains the thalamus which is a way station to the cerebrum and the hypothalamus which controls metabolism, body temperature, and so forth. The limbic system regulates emotional behavior. Parts of it seem to be related to memory storage in the cerebrum but how is still unclear. It may be that the emotional value given to incoming information determines the impression it makes in long-term memory.

The neomammalian brain is of most interest to us. It is made up of two large hemispheres connected by a structure called the corpus callosum. This structure allows them to communicate back and forth with each other through pathways called commissures. The cerebrum is responsible for voluntary movements, consciousness, personality, higher learning, sense perception, thinking, and cultural behavior. The ability to symbol lies in the cerebrum. It is somewhat like an orange in that it has an inside which accounts for most of the bulk, and an outside "peel" called the cortex. The cortex is in reality the seat of the abilities listed above. The internal white matter is connecting fiber from one area to another and to the rest of the brain.

One further part of the brain is important to us and does not belong to either of the three parts above. It has been around from the beginning and has simply enlarged as evolution progressed. This is the cerebellum. It controls body balance, muscle tone, and is important in making voluntary movements. Later in our analysis of tool use, skill is referred to as being involved with the right cerebral hemisphere. That is skill at the highest level of consciousness. In the cerebellum we have skilled *movements* controlled at their most basic levels. Coordination of movements is also partially controlled here. The cerebellum is much like a small computer for analyzing movements as they are carried out.

## MEMORY STORAGE

It is likely that there are at least two types of memory: long-term and short-term. It has been suggested that long-term memory occurs when structural changes occur in the brain. Short-term memory, on the other hand, may be dynamic and consist of either nerve impulses or slow patterns of electrical charges that wax and wane, or both. There is very good evidence that experience causes changes in the brain. Mark Rosenzweig, Edward Bennett, and Marian Cleeves (1972) have demonstrated this with rats. They raised rats in four different environments and then checked for differences in the ratio of cortex to subcortex. The standard lab environment consisted of a metal cage with three rats. The enriched environment was a large cage with twelve rats, complete with playthings, and the impoverished environment was a bare cage with one rat. They also used a seminatural environment with a dirt floor and natural features. The rats from the seminatural environment showed the greatest ratio of cortex to subcortex in weight. The other groups showed smaller ratios according to the richness of their environment, with the rats raised in isolation showing the smallest ratio of all! Here then is evidence that experience directly affects the brain. This change in the amount of cortex is probably the gross result of memory storage.

It is known that neurons, or nerve cells, do not increase in numbers after the brain has reached maturity. If a portion of the brain is destroyed by an injury or a toxin, the damage is permanent; the destroyed portion will not regenerate. It seems likely that the result of the above experiment is due to growth in that part of the neuron that carries the nerve pulse to other neurons, the axon. Greater connectivity of neurons through synapses probably results from experience.

Short-term memory may be related to images in the brain and these images to consciousness. It will take a considerable amount of research to show the relationship between the psychological experiences a person has and the anatomy and physiology of the brain that makes it possible. A number of fascinating results have already been obtained. Neurosurgeons sometimes find it necessary to remove parts of the cerebral cortex that have been damaged, causing seizures, or in some other way are abnormal. Before removing an area they may use electrodes to "map" it. In this way they can sometimes keep from removing portions important for essential movements or sensations. An interesting thing occurs when the electrode is applied. There is a delay of one-half to five seconds (Libet 1966:165-181) and then the patient may turn his head and eyes or one of his fingers may contract. He may try to speak and find himself unable to do so. By moving the electrode around and watching the result, one can map the surface of the cortex. There are some areas that are quite uniform from brain to brain such as the motor areas in Figures 4 and 5. Other areas show no response at all.

Penfield and Roberts in *Speech and Brain Mechanisms* (1959) suggest that anything which has entered the stream of consciousness is recorded in the brain. When some areas are touched with the electrode a person may re-experience (not just remember) something which happened to him in the past. He sees the image that he saw then. The conscious awareness brought on by the electrode, as said before, only comes after a delay of one-half to five seconds. It is as if a state must be set up in the brain tissue. Pribram (1971:17) has suggested that this state is a slow pulse of electricity through a field of neurons by way of ephapses which are tiny unstructured connections. This pulse is called the "slow potential microstructure" and forms what is subjectively experienced as an image.

Short-term memory probably consists of something like this "slow potential microstructure" which holds an image in the brain circuitry for a period of time during which it can be brought to consciousness. If it is important enough to the brain it may then be stored through some kind of biochemical and/or structural change. Then, when a cue from the environment or other parts of the brain touches off a state like the one set up by the electrode, one remembers with an image or word similar to the original. This is a very simple memory model but adequate for our purposes.

There are several types of learning. Man seems to share them all with other animals. These various types of learning may be only different aspects

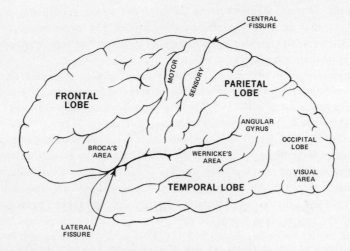

**Figure 4. Left cerebral hemispere showing lobes and areas important in normal linguistic functions.**

of the same neurophysiological process but they are not yet thoroughly understood at the neurophysiological level.

## SYMBOLS AND SIGNS

Earlier we said that culture is a body of learned behavior passed across generations. One prerequisite for culture, then, would be adequate memory storage capacity so that relatively complex learning could occur. In our discussion of hominid fossils we saw that gross cranial capacity tripled from *Australopithecus* to modern man. It is likely that the increase in the gross number of neurons increased both memory storage capacity and the ability to learn. Just the increase in size of the brain and in the number of neurons is probably not enough, however, to account for the existence of culture. We have to ask other questions. It has been said that man's ability to symbol makes him unique.

*The ability to symbol is the ability freely and arbitrarily to originate, determine, and bestow meaning upon things and events in the external world, and the ability to comprehend such meanings. These meanings cannot be grasped and appreciated with the senses. For example, holy water is not the same thing as ordinary water, and this value is meaningful and significant to millions of people. How does ordinary water become holy water? The answer is simple: human beings bestow this meaning upon it and determine its significance.* (White 1973:1)

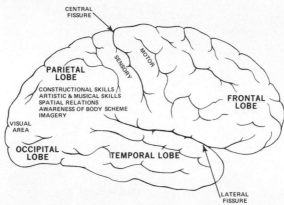

CENTRAL
FISSURE

SENSORY

MOTOR

PARIETAL
LOBE

CONSTRUCTIONAL SKILLS
ARTISTIC & MUSICAL SKILLS
SPATIAL RELATIONS
AWARENESS OF BODY SCHEME
IMAGERY

FRONTAL
LOBE

VISUAL
AREA

OCCIPITAL
LOBE

TEMPORAL LOBE

LATERAL
FISSURE

**Figure 5. Right cerebral hemispere showing lobes and
specialized functions.**

What is the neurological basis for this unique ability? How is it related to the
use of language?

Karl Pribram, an experimental neurophysiologist, feels that "two classes
of communicative Acts can be distinguished on the basis of whether the
meaning of the Act depends on the context in which it occurs." Context-free
communicative acts are labeled "signs" and context-dependent communicative acts are labeled "symbols" (Pribram 1971:305). A sign by these criteria
is a configuration that "means" the same thing regardless of the context it is
found in. A symbol draws meaning from the experiences a person has had and
the value he endowed these experiences with. To use Pribram's example,
"The sign 🌹 is a rose is a rose. The symbol 卍 has a different meaning for
the Jew than it has for the Hindu." (Ibid:332) If we are to deal with the
biological elements necessary for fully developed culture, we must look at the
ability to symbol. To understand this ability we must understand the organization of the cerebral cortex and something about how it may have evolved.

**HEMISPHERIC SPECIALIZATIONS**

When epilepsy begins to threaten a patient's life because of the frequency
or severity of seizures, an operation may be performed to split the corpus
callosum which connects the two cerebral hemispheres. This operation was
tried initially because animal studies indicated that it would be successful.
Epilepsy seems to result from the spontaneous firing of nerve impulses from
patches of injured or congenitally defective nervous tissue. Usually, this
defective tissue was found in only one of the cerebral hemispheres. The
cerebral hemispheres communicate with each other through the corpus
callosum. Thus, when a seizure begins in one hemisphere it quickly spreads to
the other. It seemed logical that by severing the connection between the

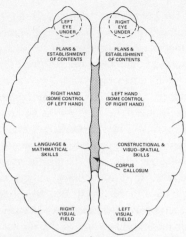

**Figure 6. View of cerebral hemispheres from above.**
**Corpus callosum is not normally exposed.**

hemispheres the seizure would be limited to one side or the other. This would leave the opposite side free to help control the body. Several of these split brain operations have been performed with moderate success. They have provided extremely useful information about mental processes. Although the patient often shows apparently normal behavior following such an operation, it has been tentatively demonstrated that there are two spheres of consciousness where before there had been one (Gazzaniga 1970:143-145).

Most right-handed people demonstrate what is known as left cerebral dominance. This means that their left cerebral hemisphere controls their right hand and that it performs the language function. When the left cerebral hemisphere is truly dominant the right hemisphere will control the left hand and will be for the most part without the ability to produce speech. It can, however, understand simple speech. Nouns tend to be recognized by the right hemisphere but not verbs. According to Lenneberg (1970:362) eighty-two people out of one hundred will be right handed and the left hemisphere will control the right hand. Handedness will not be clearly established in nine people. Three clearly right-handed individuals will show mixed or right cerebral "dominance." There will be six left handers, three with left cerebral "dominance" and three with right. In Luria's book of case histories of brain injured patients, *Traumatic Aphasia* (1970), he shows that many individuals who do not fit the usual pattern were "changed" by their parents or come from families that show pedigrees with a high percentage of left handers. Slowly, the abilities of the two hemispheres have been charted by testing split brain patients (Figures 4, 5, and 6). It may be that it is not really correct to refer to one hemisphere as dominant. The two have specialized functions. Speech is so important to us that the hemisphere with speech has been labeled dominant, but the other hemisphere may not simply be subordinate. Since we are interested in the evolution of the mechanisms which make culture possible it may be especially important that we not see the hemispheres as other than interdependent for normal functioning.

It has been known for many years that the language function is usually found in the left hemisphere. The importance of the functions of the right hemisphere is only beginning to be appreciated. This is true of course because the right hemisphere cannot communicate verbally. Psychologists and neurologists have tended to view the right hemisphere as subordinate because language was not present. It is now being suggested that very important components of thought are more highly developed in the right hemisphere than in the left (Bogen 1969-II). Perhaps one of the most important events in human evolution has been this separation of the modes of thought.

Injuries to the left hemisphere (or whichever contains the language function) produce aphasia. Aphasia is the loss of the ability to speak or the loss of the ability to understand speech or both. This will be discussed at length later. Injuries to the right hemisphere produce disturbances in the ability to recognize people, places, and objects. Patients with right hemispheric lesions may have a hard time dealing with spatial relationships. They may be unable to find their way through their own neighborhood. If they happen to be musicians or craftsmen, they may lose these abilities. Visual hallucinations are more frequent with right hemispheric injuries (Figure 5).

In patients whose cerebral hemispheres have been split apart, it is possible to examine further for specialization of function. The right hand, controlled by the left hemisphere, retains the ability to communicate through writing. It cannot, however, draw geometric figures well. The left hand cannot write well, since the right hemisphere lacks linguistic ability, but it can draw geometric figures. This picture is neither precise nor totally consistent since it has been shown that either hemisphere retains some control of the hand on its own side. The evidence is striking, however, and highly indicative. Neurologists sometimes use the term *constructional apraxia* to refer to disturbances of the ability to form geometric patterns through arranging, building, or drawing. This disturbance is more frequent in injuries to the right hemisphere and has been attributed to the inability to conceptualize spatial relationships (Bogen and Gazzaniga 1965:394-399).

The right hemisphere, then, is not a blank slate. Indeed, the realization that it may give form to otherwise linear thought has rather far-reaching implications. Here, we may see a structural correlation to many of the dualities encountered in anthropology, philosophy, psychology, and literature. (See Bogen 1969-II and Ornstein 1972 for a more complete discussion of these dualities.) We find the synthetic opposed to analytic, the propositional opposed to the imaginative, verbal to nonverbal, yin to yang, and so on. To give a concrete and extremely mundane example of opposite tacts by the different hemispheres, one split brain patient was observed by a doctor pulling his pants down with one hand and up with the other!

Specialization of function develops in the hemispheres apparently according to which side language engrams are laid down in first. When language functions start developing in one hemisphere, the other takes over spatial and perceptual functions. Early childhood injuries to the left hemisphere result in right cerebral "dominance."

The implications of this research for anthropologists and educators may be considerable. Educators have often stressed analytic skills in the form of linguistic and mathematical course content. It may be that the synthetic, spatial component in the higher forms of learning is extremely important, yet, who has taken a how-to course on image production in the brain? (Here and in the figures "image" is not used in the strict sense in which neuro-psychologists would use it. It is used interchangeably with "imagery" and refers to primarily nonverbal, pictorial components of thought.) On a less *avant garde* level, who has taken a course on three-dimensional perception? Henry Moore, a sculptor, has suggested that most people never fully develop this ability. He says:

*This is what the sculptor must do. He must strive continually to think of, and use form in its full spatial completeness. He gets the solid shape, as it were, inside his head—he thinks of it, whatever its size, as if he were holding it completely enclosed in the hollow of his hand. He mentally visualizes a complex form from all round itself; he knows while he looks at one side what the other side is like; he identifies himself with its center of gravity, its mass, its weight; he realizes its volume, as the space that the shape displaces in the air.* (Moore 1961:74)

It is quite possible that not only artistic creation but scientific investigation draws upon the synthetic imagery of the right cerebral hemisphere. Konrad Lorenz suggests that this may be the process usually known as intuition:

*. . .very probably all scientific discoveries of laws of nature are primarily guided by the discoverer's gestalt perception. The first sign that the perception of a lawfulness is beginning to stand out against the background of the "white noise" of chaotic accidental data is that the phenomena in which it prevails begin to assume a quite particular, if as yet quite undefinable, and intriguingly attractive quality. The potential discoverer finds himself irresisti-*

*bly compelled to occupy himself with the phenomena in question and quite automatically to gather more and more information about them until, often quite suddenly, the gestalt of the suspected lawfulness stands out from the background of accidental data with such convincing clarity that one wonders how one could have overlooked it for such a long time.* (1969:41)

## TOOL USE AND THE BRAIN

Anthropologists have long speculated about the importance of tool use and tool manufacture in hominid evolution. Analyzing tool use and manufacture in terms of cerebral specialization gives new insight into the nature of this ability (Figure 7). We have already referred to the right hand's inability to copy geometric figures accurately (though handwriting is intact) in split brain patients, yet the right hand in a normal right-handed person is the one that is used in tasks requiring skill. This result is consistent with the observation that injuries to the right hemisphere often destroy artistic ability and craftsmanship. The left hand in split brain patients functions almost as usual except that it cannot write even crudely since the right hemisphere has little linguistic ability. Why is normal function for skilled construction channeled through the left hemisphere to the right hand? This question cannot be answered with certainty, but there are tantilizing hints.

The right cerebral hemisphere understands only simple language. It best understands noun-object words and secondarily adjectives. Verbs are not understood (Gazzaniga 1970:119). Verbs used as nouns such as "jump" in, "He got the jump on her," are likewise not recognized. Verbs express action;

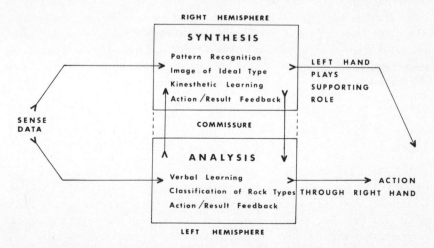

Figure 7. Tool use flow chart showing interaction of cerebral hemisperes in normal functioning.

it is hard to imagine a consciousness without the ability to understand action symbols, but the right hemisphere has just that type of consciousness. Verbs are necessary to represent cause and effect. The left hemisphere is the more analytic then, at least partially because it can process symbolic information that deals with action and cause and effect sequences. It would seem important that man's most skilled hand be controlled by the hemisphere that best understands cause and effect.

Which came first, the skill or the hemispheric specialization? Since the above argument is somewhat circular, this must be our next question. This dilemma is solved by realizing that "which came first" questions are often not answerable as either/or when we are dealing with evolution. The whole complex of increasing verbal ability, skilled tool use and manufacture, and lateral cerebral specialization likely evolved together.

One can imagine that tool manufacture might take place as schematized in Figure 7. A material is selected according to a classification system that is the result of experience and perhaps social learning. This system may consist of a cognitive scheme:

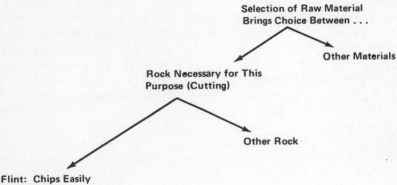

A similar set of choices may be made for size and shape of the flint to be used. The right hemisphere may contribute to this decision with its "feel" for ideal shape and size that has resulted from kinesthetic learning and perception of dimensions and angles. Further imagine a running commentary from the verbal side, "Yes, that one is the right shape but too thin; last one that thin broke." We have the hemispheres supplementing each other in the selecting procedure. After the choice is made they will further supplement each other in construction. The left hand will hold and the right will begin the action necessary for manufacture controlled primarily by the action-oriented left hemisphere. The right hemisphere has a small amount of direct control but its skill will be constantly drawn upon by the left hemisphere through the cerebral commissures that connect them. Both hemispheres will take part in producing the final shape, "That last blow was a bit hard (match of present shape to ideal shape takes place in other hemisphere), a little more will have to come off the other side to make it balance." Electrode exploration of the cortex has shown (Figure 6) that the motor control area for the right hand is on the left hemisphere. Yet, information from the right hemisphere must come through the commissures and participate in the process of tool manufacture, or an inferior tool will result.

## LANGUAGE AND THE BRAIN

Before examining further the possible evolution of hemispheric specialization, let us look at the hemisphere that is usually referred to as the dominant hemisphere. Here rests the true phylogenetic apex of human ability: language.

Eric Lenneberg (1969) has listed five reasons for suspecting that language is to a certain extent "built into" man's brain. These can be altered to suit current knowledge:

1. There are anatomical and physiological specializations in man's brain and speech apparatus specific for language. There are, for example, special areas of the cortex concerned with the production of speech. Cerebral "dominance" may well be related to language function. When the size of the human brain is less than that of some apes in microcephalic adults, these individuals still communicate passably though they are usually of low intelligence (Holloway 1968:126-128). This suggests that brain volume alone is not enough; human brains are organized differently from ape brains.

2. Speech onset is regular and follows a fixed sequence. Principles of categorization rather than specific items are learned. These principles are the same cross-culturally.

3. There is a difficulty in suppressing language to the extent that blindness, deafness, and extreme parental neglect may fail to prevent the development of some form of linguistic ability.

4. Language has not been taught to other species in its full complexity. It now appears possible that chimpanzees may be able to learn more than one hundred "words" consisting of hand signs or bits of shaped plastic and use these to construct sentences. It is still unknown how well two chimps could communicate in this fashion and whether one chimp could teach another. The complexity of this chimp language is certainly far removed from human language but its very difference may prove illustrative for *Homo sapiens*.

5. Even though some languages seem unrelated through history they still

show universal principles. These principles may be semantic, related to meaning, they may be phonological, related to sound, or they may be related to sentence structure or syntax.

What is the nature of language in the developed brain? Quite a bit of knowledge has accumulated from studies of aphasic patients which allows a tentative, elementary answer to this question. When the cerebral hemisphere with the language function is damaged and language is disturbed this disturbance is called aphasia. A Frenchman, Paul Broca, first pointed out the fact that damage to a specific area of the brain could produce a specific language disturbance. His first paper was written in 1861. Since that time large numbers of aphasics have been studied and much has been learned about the language areas.

There are several steps in the reception, understanding of, and production of speech. Speech sounds must be picked up by the ears of the receiver and these stimuli referred to a receiving area. From the receiving area, the incoming message must be endowed with meaning by memories associated with the sound. If the person responds with a sentence of his own, these associations must be sorted and put into sentence form and the speech apparatus, i.e., lips, tongue, jaw, and so forth must then be controlled in such a way that speech is produced. This is a simplex view of a complex process, but this is the level of analysis available with the present state of knowledge.

When aphasia patients have injuries in the vicinity of Wernicke's area (Figure 4) They have trouble understanding language. They seem to be unable to analyze sound patterns. This is known as acoustic aphasia. The production of speech is usually not impaired by this type of injury. This indicates that this is a receiving area in which heard speech is initially processed. Injuries to the angular gyrus region of the cortex produce a semantic aphasia. The angular gyrus region is an association area. Auditory output from Wernicke's area seems to associate with visual patterns here. When the language input is visual in reading, the visual area refers information to the angular gyrus which then refers it to Wernicke's area where it is put into auditory form (Geschwind 1972:79). If the words are to be spoken, the auditory forms will be referred back through the angular gyrus and through the arcuate fasciculus to Broca's area. Broca's area will produce the spoken words by commanding a proper coordinated response from the muscles involved in the production of speech. An injury to Broca's area, then, results in a production aphasia. A patient with this type of aphasia can understand speech but cannot produce it.

A number of linguists have suggested that language learning is a special type of rapid learning called imprinting that we discussed earlier. Imprinting usually occurs in younger animals at a seemingly extra sensitive period. It is irreversible and may occur without reward. All this simply says that imprinting is rapid and, in environments that are not grossly abnormal, it is certain. Language learning seems to fit this pattern.

To suggest that language learning is possible and even highly likely because of innate propensities does not imply that specific content is innate. A child will learn whatever language he hears in the society in which he grows up. Man's brain is simply "wired" in such a way that it is highly likely that some language will be learned.

Ignatius Mattingly has suggested that speech evolved as "sign stimuli" from a call system. Most primates have some kind of repertoire of calls that they make at appropriate times. He feels that during the course of hominid evolution an "intellect capable of making a semantic representation of the world of experience" evolved in conjunction with a "phonetic social releaser system a reliable and rapid carrier of information" (1972:335). He is saying that man developed the capability of distinguishing objects and actions and their meaning for him beyond that of other animals. Stereoscopic color vision and the ability to pick up and manipulate objects with the hands probably added to this ability. Concurrently, a system of calls was being elaborated and associated with objects and actions. These calls were imprinted, not innate, and thus a large number could be used and given meaning in the daily routine. Being picked up by imprinting in infancy was sure, quick, and less determined and more adaptable than being rigidly inherited.

Gordon Hewes (1971) who has worked extensively with theories of language origin feels that earlier language consisted mostly of gestures. *Australopithecus* may have had fifty or more. We have seen already how flirting behavior may be built in in man. It is conceivable that a number of other nonverbal signs could have been used in specific situations. Calls would likely have accompanied some of these gestures. Later as selection occurred for an increase in information-processing capacity, an imprinting mechanism for sounds could have evolved.

Noam Chomsky, a well-known and often quoted linguist (1967, 1959), feels that linguistic ability is a highly specific faculty resulting from man's genetic endowment. This faculty shows itself in the general principles that determine rules of grammar in different languages. He calls these general principles "deep structures" and sees them as being similar for all languages. The "surface structures" that are generated from these principles become more specific for the language spoken the further they are from the deep structure. Eric Lenneberg (1969:368) has even suggested that the deep structures for language and algebra are the same.

The nature/nurture argument has found its way into linguistic behavior. In 1957 B. F. Skinner wrote a book called *Verbal Behavior* in which he tried to account for language learning as operant conditioning. The book was criticized by Chomsky in a journal review (1959:26-58). The debate between the two schools continued for several years. Many linguists now assume that, as usual, it is not an either/or question. Early learning of a language probably takes place through imprinting. Most people, however, continue to learn new words and language skills throughout their adult lives. Later learning likely follows the Skinnerian model.

As we have seen, there are specific areas of the brain that are concerned with particular aspects of language. How have these evolved and what do they have to do with man's ability to symbol? Since Wernicke's area is where initial processing takes place, it is most likely the locality where speech is perceived as "sign stimuli." We have already discussed this.

The angular gyrus region is a kind of "association area of association areas." It may be implicated in the ease of human language learning. Geschwind (1972) has championed the view that man is able to associate memories from one area of the cortex directly with memories from other areas. Man probably does this much more easily than other primates who must associate one area of the cortex through lower structures of the brain and back to the cortex. Apes do have some ability to do this (Davenport and Rogers 1970:279-280). The angular gyrus region performs this function. A perceived word is associated with auditory memories in Wernicke's area, then referred to the angular gyrus. It is then associated with visual memories as mentioned before in the visual cortex and referred back through the angular gyrus, then forward to Broca's area for a spoken response. The angular gyrus region may represent one area that has been "restructured" in hominid evolution to serve a language function.

A consideration of Broca's area brings us to an exciting piece of research carried out by Lieberman et al. Broca's area is adjacent to the area that controls the muscles of speech and probably coordinates these muscles to produce speech. Think for a moment about the complex movements necessary to utter a single identical syllable over and over. What kind of selection would have been necessary to produce not only the speech apparatus but this marvelous coordinating mechanism? Lieberman and his colleagues (1972:287,307) have tried to answer this question. There are three resonating chambers in the human vocal tract that modify the frequency of sound produced by the larynx (Hill 1972:309). Lieberman has examined the chimpanzee vocal tract as well as the reconstructed vocal tract of Neanderthal and modeled sound production for these by use of a computer model. His results suggest the vowels *a*, *i*, and *u* were difficult or impossible for Neanderthal to make just as they are impossible for a human infant and chimpanzee. He feels that this suggests a linguistic ability for Neanderthal inferior to that of modern man. Neanderthal, according to him, probably communicated slowly and inefficiently. This probably means that the neurological and vocal elements necessary for speech production evolved together rather than one preceding the other.

## THE BRAIN AND HUMAN NATURE

We have now surveyed the two cerebral hemispheres and had a brief and limited look at some of their special functions. What does the existence of specialization in these two hemispheres tell us? How did they come to have specialized functions and how have these specialties been important in cultural evolution? Are these specializations important in forming culture? What, indeed, is the ability to symbol? All of these questions are key questions in physical anthropology and it will take extensive research and theoretical work to answer them. Since we have surveyed some of the data, however, it will be fun to speculate.

It may be that anthropologists have been searching too hard for single factor explanations of lateral specialization in the brain. Selection for tool use or for linguistic ability has been used as the explanation. The two have been often seen as two facets of the same ability. We have seen, however, that true skill rests not in the left hemisphere with the language function but in the right hemisphere. Though the left hemisphere controls the right hand, it must draw upon the object knowledge of the right hemisphere through the commissures. It was suggested that this is the case because the right hemisphere is not as knowledgeable about action as the left. The left understands action because it can proposition. It thinks in terms of subjects and predicates. In the last century John Hughlings Jackson (Taylor 1958) suggested, "Both halves are alike in so far as each contains processes for words. They are unlike in that the left alone is for use of words in speech and the right for other processes in which words serve."

There is experimental evidence that the two hemispheres interfere with each other in the performance of their specialized tasks. Thus, a person can balance a wooden dowel for a longer period in his left hand if he is repeating nonsense syllables than if he is silent (Kinsbourne and Cook 1971:341-345). The right hemisphere is uninterrupted in directing the balancing because the left hemisphere is attending to a chore it understands. How much more interruption of function would take place if the hemispheres were not specialized? Looking at the problem in this way and seeing a selection for tool use and gesture language occurring concurrently with a selection for better linguistic ability, why not suppose that these functions started to separate? Chimpanzees also show handedness. Meager data indicates about an even preference for right and left hands (Finch 1941:117-118). Handedness in chimps probably represents an early stage in the process of lateral specialization congruent with their ability to use tools. Not all show a preference. Songbirds have hemispheric lateralization, as one might expect considering their elaborate repertoires (Nottebohm 1970:950-956). As gesture language became conscious it would have become part of the right hemisphere's function just like tool use; body-scheme awareness occupies the angular gyrus region on the right side. This model of cerebral specialization solves many of the problems entailed in seeing the left hemisphere as a dominant hemisphere responsible for both language and tool use. The increased efficiency in brain function plus the growing ability to communicate and use tools could partially explain man's rapid evolution during the Pleistocene.

In this light we will look again at man's ability to symbol. Is man's ability to symbol no more, perhaps, than his ability to make propositions superimposed upon an already superior primate intelligence? Such intelligence has been demonstrated especially by chimpanzees both in the wild and in experiments. Bernard Rensch discovered in one experiment (1972:85-87) that a chimp could solve terrifically complex mazes. She seemed to attack the problem by visualizing in advance the correct solution and then acting. Human subjects attacked the problem in the same way. While they beat the chimp in most cases, they sometimes took longer than she. The ability to delay a response while working on possible solutions may tell us something. Rensch (Ibid:87-89) also feels that chimps have a budding ego or awareness of self. Other researchers have observed this with chimps. Washoe, the chimp taught to "speak" gesture language, was tested directly on this by being asked of her reflection, "Who is that?" She responded, "Me, Washoe" (Gardner and Gardner 1971). Awareness of self may be the prerequisite for the primal subject in sentences. The aware ego can delay its actions and know that it acts. The awareness of action then becomes the primal predicate and, "I do," the first complete sentence.

The ability to symbol in man is undoubtedly involved with frontal lobe function. It is there that the propensity to organize, sort, and classify lies. It is the frontal lobe function to establish the context from which symbols derive meaning. Says Pribram, "Symbols derive meaning by establishing a context within which interests, feelings become organized. Signs intend some part of the World-Out-There. Symbols refer to occurrences in the domain of the organism's World-Within" (1971:351). Individuals can lead almost normal lives with nonfunctional frontal lobes. They lose the ability, however, to divorce their actions from the immediate situation they find themselves in. The highest cognitive capacity of establishing a context for behavior beyond the response to the stimuli of the moment is impossible. The frontal cortex is phylogenetically one of the latest additions to the brain. For this reason, it has been called the social brain. It is also one of the latest maturing structures of the brain and one of the most easily damaged. Sociogenic damage of this type has far-reaching implications for public policy; such damage may turn out to be rather common (Munro 1972; Montagu 1972).

Man's highest mental functions are all interrelated as we have already seen. His left hemisphere permits his communication with other minds in a complex symbolic code. It understands action and acts to shape man's world. It cannot act to create to its fullest extent without borrowing the understanding of objects, three-dimensional space, imagery, and perception of overall patterns provided by the right hemisphere. Finally, holy water becomes more than ordinary water because man can say, "The water is holy." This is quite different from saying, "The rose is a rose is a rose." It is expressing one thing in terms of another. The water is endowed with the quality, holiness. This quality gets its reality not from the external world but from the context provided by the frontal lobe function of placing value on experience. All a person's religious experiences form the contextual category within which the water becomes holy.

# Biocultural Evolution and Hominization II

For a few moments let us pretend that we can stand far away and see the whole course of hominid evolution spread out before us. Though cultural evolution and biological evolution begin as one and are interwoven thereafter, we will also pretend that we can represent each as a line. We can then chart the course of each relative to the other, through time across the page and increasing in complexity up the page. We will start the lines with *Australopithecus* and end them at the present. Then, we will start again and try to project them a short distance into the future: all the time we will assume for the sake of harmony that ecotastrophe, global war, and the other specters of our century will be averted (Figure 8).

During the period represented by the two lines, beginning three million years ago and stretching to perhaps 400,000 years ago, the lines run almost parallel. Culturally, no startling amount of change takes place. Change consists mostly of developing the cutting edge on stone tools and moving more toward construction and away from finding and using. Biologically, the size of the brain doubles. Language ability probably increases from a small number to a larger number of gestures, perhaps fifty to a thousand (Hewes 1971). Vocal communication consisting of complex calls likely increases in relation to the number of gestures used toward the end of the period. Organized hunting has become progressively more important throughout.

In the next 300,000 years cultural and biological evolution are still roughly parallel in their rates of change. Shape becomes important in tools at about the same time that complex vocal units develop, with multiple sounds being used together in "sentences." Towards the end of the period new tool techniques develop; they are constructed in multiple stages. The brain has increased by another 50 percent in size and much of the restructuring that will occur has occurred.

By 100,000 years ago the brain has reached its maximum size. Verbal communication is fully established but is slow and broken. Hunting is a way of life. Tools are still being refined. All of these trends continue until about thirty thousand years ago with the rise of truly modern *Homo sapiens.* Art

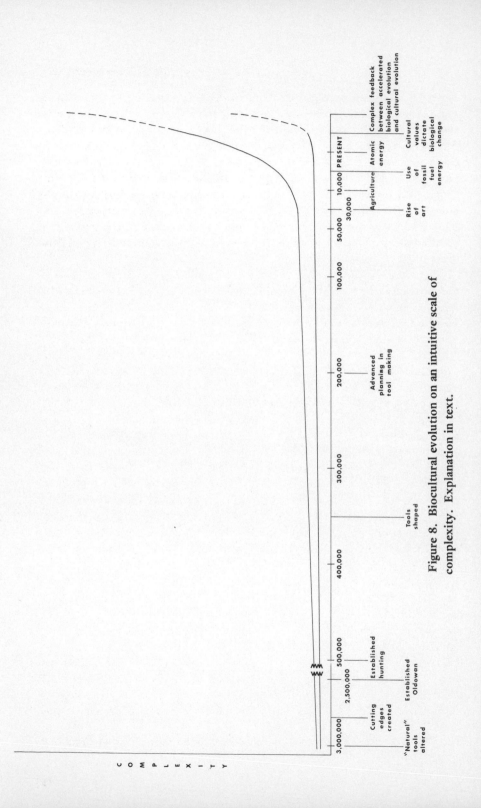

Figure 8. Biocultural evolution on an intuitive scale of complexity. Explanation in text.

begins. At this point, cultural evolution is suddenly progressing at a much more rapid rate than biological evolution. Biological evolution remains constant or slows. Between ten thousand and fifteen thousand years ago, agriculture develops. Man is producing his own food and city life begins. The line representing culture is climbing rapidly away from the biological base line. There are two rapid increases in the rate of change in the last thirty thousand years. One comes with the advent of agriculture and the other with the beginning of the industrial revolution and the use of fossil fuel energy. Our perspective is so broad, however, that these events are not even seen in the accelerated rate of culture change. This brings us to the present, the use of atomic energy, and space travel.

This very brief coverage of biocultural evolution only provides us with the most important events in hominid evolution. These events are covered in depth in most textbooks (See Kelso 1970, for example.) The assignment of specific time periods for these stages is arbitrary. For our purposes, however, this schematic presentation is adequate. The scale of complexity in Figure 8 is intuitive, not because biological and cultural complexity cannot be quantified, but because the topic is so complex and lengthy as to require a monograph. Anyone interested should refer to Naroll and von Bertalanffy (1956), Schaefer (1969), or Lomax and Berkowitz (1972).

We will break the time scale of biocultural evolution into four parts. The first ended when culture change was no longer propelled primarily by the selection for behavioral genetic characters in a feedback relationship to culture. This probably occurred with the first art thirty thousand years ago, though any given beginning is arbitrary since we are not talking about an abrupt change. The second period begins there and ends at the present time. During this period, cultural change greatly outstrips biological change due to the interaction of symbolic elements. Our present culture has become sophisticated enough technologically and bold enough socially to begin "intervening" in biological evolution. Cultural values may soon dictate biological change. This will bring stage three. Tangentially, technological man has altered the course of biological evolution already through ignorance of the effects of pollution. Our whole scheme depends, as previously suggested, on the usual qualifications based on the fragile ecological and social conditions now threatening man. The reference here is to cultural man bringing about changes directly in biological man. The fourth period will begin after the above step has been taken and a condition of feedback between biological and cultural evolution holds once again. We might call this "hominization II" since once again biocultural interactions become important.

We have already discussed at some length the biocultural changes that occurred in the first period. The second period is typified by a great elaboration of elements due to the interaction of symbols and concepts. Concept "A" interacts with concept "B" to become a new combination, "C." "C" then interacts with other concepts to form further configurations, and so on. We illustrated this interaction previously with the laser beam example. Cultural anthropologists have a number of different theoretical perspectives on these processes. White, for example, uses the term symbolate to refer to this phenomenon. The third period has begun. It came into being with modern genetics, and one can probably safely predict that it will end with this century.

It is now possible to seriously consider "gene therapy" for the 1500 known human genetic diseases. "Concurrent with the recent progress toward biochemical characterization of human genetic diseases have been [sic] the dramatic advance in our understanding of the structure and function of the genetic material, DNA, and our ability to manipulate it in the test tube" (Friedmann and Roblin 1972:949). The ability to manipulate DNA is not likely, however, to remain in the test tube. It is now possible to consider genetic surgery. Specific genes would be located in human DNA. The genetic code of the gene would be duplicated except for the part to be changed. The original gene would then be burned out using a laser beam. Later in the developmental process, substitute DNA would be introduced by way of an artificial virus. Or it will be possible to "turn off" genes in the developing organism by chemical means and introduce new ones the same way.

Imagine for a moment what might happen if it becomes possible to easily and efficiently change the intelligence of the next generation through genetic manipulation. Would it be done? Probably. How would it change our culture? One obvious possibility would be the creation of a stratified society in which the younger, more intelligent generation passes out early retirements to their subhuman creators. This is an extreme example, but suggestive of the unpredictability of biocultural interactions. By our own scheme, new intensive feedback relationships between culture and biology would signify the beginning of our fourth period. While it is interesting and exciting to talk about the fourth period of biocultural evolution, we will leave it to the futurologists. The point has been made. It is not likely that we can predict with any accuracy what form these interactions will take. The biocultural feedback that produced *Homo sapiens* may produce super man—or worse!

# References
# Cited

Bielicki, T. 1969. "Deviation-amplifying cybernetic systems and hominid evolution." *Materialy i Prace Anthropologicyne* 77:57-60.

Bogen, J. E. 1969. "The other side of the brain, I, II, III." *Bulletin of the Los Angeles Neurological Societies* 34, No. 3 (Part III with G. M. Bogen).

Bogen, J. E., and Gazzaniga, M. S. 1965. "Cerebral commissurotomy in man: Minor hemisphere dominance for certain visio-spatial functions." *Journal of Neurosurgery* 23:349-399.

Bowlby, J. 1969. *Attachment and Loss.* Vol. 1: *Attachement.* London: Hogarth Press.

Broca, P. 1861. "Remarques sur la siège de la faculté du langage articulé, suivies d'une observation d'aphemie (perte de la parole)." *Bulletins de la Société Anatomique de Paris.* Tome VI, 36:330-357.

Calhoun, J. B. 1956. "A comparative study of two inbred strains of house mice." *Ecological Monographs* 26:81-103.

Chomsky, N. 1967. *Language and mind.* New York: Harcourt, Brace and World.

———. 1959. "Review of Skinner's verbal behavior." *Language* XXXV:26-58.

Darwin, C. 1859. *The origin of species by means of natural selection.* London: John Murray.

Davenport, R. D., and Rogers, C. M. 1970. "Intermodal equivalence of stimuli in apes." *Science* 168:279-280.

Eible-Eibesfeldt, I. 1970. *Ethology: The biology of behavior.* New York: Holt, Rinehart and Winston.

Erlenmeyer-Kimling, L., and Jarvik, L. 1963. "Genetics and intelligence: A review." *Science* 1942:1477-79. Reprinted in *Behavioral genetics: Method and research.* M. Manosevitz et al., eds. New York: Appleton-Century-Crofts, 1969.

Finch, G. 1941. "Chimpanzee handedness." *Science* 94:117-118.

Fisher, E. M. 1939. "Habits of the southern sea otter." *Journal of Mammalogy* 20:21-36.

Friedmann, T., and Roblin, R. 1972. "Gene therapy for human genetic disease?" *Science* 175:949-955.

Gardner, A. R., and Gardner, B. T. 1969. "Teaching sign language to a chimpanzee." *Science* 165:664-672.

Gardner, B. T., and Gardner, A. R. 1971. "Two way communication with an infant chimpanzee." In *Behavior of nonhuman primates,* Vol. 3. Shrier, A., and Stollnitz, F., eds. New York: Academic Press.

Gazzaniga, M. S. 1970. *The bisected brain.* New York: Appleton-Century-Crofts.

Geschwind, N. 1972. "Language and the brain." *Scientific American* 226 (4): 76-83.

Hewes, G. 1971. *Language origins: A bibliography.* Boulder: Department of Anthropology, University of Colorado.

Hill, J. G. 1972. "On the evolutionary foundations of language." *American Anthropologist* 74:308-317.

Holloway, R. 1968. "The evolution of the primate brain: Some aspects of quantitative relations." *Brain Research* 7:121-172.

Howell, F. C. 1965. *Early man.* New York: Time-Life Books.

Kawai, M. 1965. "Newly acquired precultural behavior of the troop of Japanese monkeys on Koshima islet." *Primates* 6:1-30.

Kelso, A. J. 1970. *Physical anthropology.* New York: J. B. Lippincott Co.

Kinsbourne, M., and Cook, J. 1971. "Generalized and lateralized effects of concurrent verbalization on a unimanual skill." *Quarterly Journal of Experimental Psychology* 23:341-345.

Lamarck, J. B. 1914. *Zoological philosophy.* London: Macmillan (translation of *Philosophie zoologique* originally published in Paris in 1809).

Lawick-Goodall, Jane van. 1967. *My friends the wild chimpanzees.* Washington, D. C.: National Geographic Society.

Lenneberg, E. H. 1970. "Brain correlates of language." In *The neurosciences: Second study program.* F. O. Schmitt et al., eds. New York: Rockefeller University Press.

———. 1969. "A biological perspective on language." In *Evolutionary anthropology.* H. Bleibtreu, ed. Boston: Allyn and Bacon.

Libet, B. 1966. "Brain stimulation and conscious experience." In *Brain and conscious experience.* J. C. Eccles, ed., pp. 165-181. New York: Springer-Verlag.

Lieberman, P.; Crelin, E. S.; and Klatt, D. 1972. "Phonetic ability and related anatomy of the newborn and adult human, Neanderthal man, and the chimpanzee." *American Anthropolgist* 74:287-307.

Locke, J. 1690. *Essay concerning human understanding.* Oxford: Clarendon Press.

Lomax, A., and Berkowitz, N. 1972. "The evolutionary taxonomy of culture." *Science* 177:228-239.

Lorenz, K. 1970. *Studies in animal and human behavior*. Cambridge, Mass: Harvard University Press.

———. 1969. "Innate bases of learning." In *On the biology of learning*. K. Pribram, ed. New York: Harcourt, Brace and World.

———. 1966. *On aggression*. New York: Harcourt, Brace, and World.

———. 1965. *Evolution and modification of behavior*. Chicago: Chicago University Press.

Luria, A. R. 1970. *Traumatic aphasia*. The Hague: Mouton.

McDougall, W. 1923. *An introduction to social psychology*. 15th ed. Boston: J. W. Luce.

MacLean, P. D. 1968. "Alternative neural pathways to violence." In *Alternatives to violence, a stimulus to dialogue*. New York: Time-Life Books.

Manosevitz, M.; Lindsey, G.; and Thiessen, D. D. 1969. *Behavioral genetics: Method and research*. New York: Appleton-Century-Crofts.

Mattingly, I. 1972. "Speech cues and sign stimuli." *American Scientist* 60 (3):327-337.

Montagu, A. 1972. "Sociogenic brain damage." *American Anthropologist* 74 (5): 1045-1061.

Moore, H. 1961. "Notes on sculptures." In *The creative process*. B. Ghiselin, ed. New York: Mentor Books.

Munro, N. 1972. Unpublished grant proposal. University of Montana.

Naroll, R. S., and Bertalanffy, L. von, 1956. "The principle of allometry in biology and the social sciences." In *General systems yearbook*. Bertalanffy, L. von, and Pappaport, A., eds. Washington, D.C.: Society for General Systems Research.

Nottebohn, F. 1970. "Ontogeny of bird song." *Science* 167:950-956.

Ornstein, R. E. 1972. *The psychology of consciousness*. San Francisco: W. H. Freeman & Co.

Penfield, W., and Roberts, L. 1959. *Speech and brain mechanisms*. Princeton, N. J.: Princeton University Press.

Pfeiffer, J. E. 1972. *The emergence of man*. New York: Harper and Row.

Premack, A. J., and Premack, D. D. 1972. "Teaching language to an ape." *Scientific American* 227 (4):92-99.

Pribram, K. H. 1971. *Language of the brain*. Englewood Cliffs, N. J.: Prentice-Hall.

Rensch, B. 1972. *From man to demigod*. New York: Columbia University Press.

Rosenzweig, M.; Bennett, E.; and Cleeves, M. 1972. "Brain changes in response to experience." *Scientific American* 226 (2):22-29.

Sackett, G. P. 1966. "Monkeys reared in isolation with pictures as visual input." *Science* 154:1468-1473.

Schaefer, J. M. 1969. "A comparison of three measures of social complexity." *American Anthropologist* 71:706-708.

Skinner, B. F. 1971. *Beyond freedom and dignity.* New York: Alfred A. Knopf.

———. 1961. *Cumulative record.* New York: Appleton-Century-Crofts.

———. 1957. *Verbal behavior.* New York: Appleton-Century-Crofts.

———. 1953. *Science and human behavior.* New York: Macmillan Co.

———. 1938. The Behavior of organisms. New York: Appleton-Century-Crofts.

Slater, E., and Cowie, V. 1971. *The genetics of mental disorders.* London: Oxford University Press.

Spitz, R. A., and Wolf, K. M. 1946. "The smiling response: A contribution to the ontogenesis of social relations." *General Psychological Monographs* 34:57-125.

Struhsaker, T. T., and Hunkler, P. 1971. "Evidence of tool-using by chimpanzees in the Ivory Coast." *Folia Primatologica* 15:212-219.

Taylor, J., ed. 1958. *Selected writings of John Hughlings Jackson.* New York: Basic Books.

Thiessen, D. D. 1972. *Gene organization and behavior.* New York: Random House.

Tiger, L., and Fox, R. 1971. *The imperial animal.* New York: Holt, Rinehart and Winston.

Tinbergen, N. 1951. *The study of instinct.* London: Oxford University Press.

Tobias, P. V. 1971. *The brain in hominid evolution.* New York: Columbia University Press.

Tryon, R. C. 1940. "Genetic differences in maze learning in rats." Nat. Soc. Stud. Education 39th-Yearbook, Part 1: 111-119. Bloomington, Ill. Public School Publishing Co.

Tylor, E. B. 1971. *Primitive culture.* London: John Murray.

Watson, J. B. 1930. *Behaviorism.* New York: Norton.

White, L., with Dillingham, B. 1973. *The concept of culture.* Minneapolis: Burgess Publishing Co.